Front Cover: Class C15 4-4-2T No 67474 climbs to Glen Douglas on 15 June 1959 while working the Arrochar to Craigendoran service: a photograph obtained with a little help from an unknown friend!

Back Cover: Killin station yard in 1958, presided over by 0-4-4T No 55222 in the foreground and the Grampian Mountains in the background.

Right: Ex-GNSR No 49 *Gordon Highlander* at King Edward on the Macduff branch in June 1960.

On Scottish Lines

Derek Penney

Ian Allan
PUBLISHING

First published 1999

ISBN 0 7110 2653 X

Published by Ian Allan Publishing

an imprint of Ian Allan Publishing Ltd, Terminal House, Shepperton, Surrey TW17 8AS.
Printed by Ian Allan Printing Ltd, Riverdene Business Park, Hersham, Surrey KT12 4RG.

Code: 9906/C

Introduction

In a camera shop, too 'old-fashioned' even in the 1950s to have survived today, the youth I was eagerly scanned the bundle of contact-prints that had just been exchanged for an unexpectedly frightening amount of good money. They were, I suppose, no better than one had the right to expect from a time-worn Box Brownie, a recently discovered heirloom of sorts, that had accompanied me on a recent 'loco-spotting' visit to Scotland. Little had been expected of the camera other than to provide proof beyond dispute of having rubbed shoulders with the likes of *Lord James of Douglas* and the *Baron of Bradwardine* to timid stay-at-homes with their commonplace cronies *Prince George* and *Princess Mary*. But my heart leapt with joy as I turned up, among the camera shaky, the not-quite-all-on, and the double-exposures, a precious few that had — perhaps accidentally — come out well enough to bear slight comparison with those tiny reproductions that appeared in the Ian Allan 'ABCs'. It was the beginning of the end for 'spotting', and the start of those highly enjoyable, but penurious, years that led eventually to the gathering of the photographs that appear in these pages.

Shortly afterwards, those fledgling efforts were to provide another link with what follows, when, having begun work at the Yorkshire Engine Company, I showed them, with suitable diffidence, to my first mentor there, a rosy-cheeked old boy with a vastly extended smokebox, who had charge of the oldest machines in the factory — by Sharp, Stewart of 1865 — as well as the newest apprentice. Dishearteningly, his exploration of the pictures was a little impatient, allowing only that there were 'a few good'uns', yet he was clearly on the look-out for something in particular. It was a poor thing indeed that ended his search: a broadside view, dimly lit and with the front buffer beam 'off-camera', of ex-LNER Class C15 4-4-2T No 67469. Setting aside all but this one, he brought out the ancient, dog-eared pocket book, lovingly handled as always, which contained — I imagine I was never allowed to see — well-nigh half a century's trade secrets. Nestling between its fragile pages was a postcard-sized photograph, yellowed with age, of North British Railway No 1, brand-new in works livery and quite clearly sister to the locomotive I had snapped at Dunfermline. It turned out that these engines — known, he assured me, as 'Yorkies' — were built at YEC early in his working life, and he was highly delighted they were still in use. Long after I had left his tutelage, at any chance encounter in the works he would ritually plant his feet apart, bar my way with arms akimbo and ask, nay, demand: 'Hast tha seen any more o' them theer Yorkie tanks?' Incidentally, I may be wrong but I believe this was well before Rowntree of York applied the sobriquet to a rather more ubiquitous product!

Just two 'C15s' survived long enough for me to record them on colour film, but not before old Teddy had retired, for it was about six years and half-a-dozen cameras later that I began photographing trains in colour. The pictures shown here, in roughly chronological order, date from between 1958 and 1966 and, perforce, embody a personal rather than an all-embracing view of Scotland's railways; limited opportunity as an occasionally-visiting Sassenach, capricious weather and, let's face it, personal predilections have ensured this. None the less, I am able to include scenes on the lines of all five Scottish pre-Grouping companies, although by this time locomotives of only two of them, the Caledonian and the North British, survived in regular service. Luckily, (though not forgetting *City of Truro* on the Western) it was the Scottish Region of BR that led the way in operating restored locomotives on special trains for both enthusiasts and the wider public, a policy that enables me to include at least token examples of motive power of both the Highland and the Great North of Scotland railways. It may seem like cheating to feature several pictures of the four 'restored' locomotives, but I would argue that they were such a familiar part of the Scottish rail scene during my period that it would be absurd to exclude them; all the more so since their activities have long passed into history following their permanent domiciling in the museum at Coplawhill. All of that, plus the fact that they made such lovely pictures! Similar hesitations over the inclusion of certain 'railtour' scenes have also been overcome whenever they are thought to be of exceptional interest. But no such apologia is offered in respect of what may perhaps be thought a surfeit of pictures of the ex-LNER Pacifics: that's personal predilection for you! Besides, they *were* the 'hottest ticket in town' during their final seasons for enthusiasts of all loyalties and persuasions.

Again I return to those early snapshots, long-forgotten until preparing this book, for the remembrance they evoke of first coming under the spell of Scotland and its railways. It steals over one, I fancy, by an aggregation of small incidents and experiences, trivial in themselves but collectively making up the feeling one has for time and place. Perhaps it is the rush of sweetly different-smelling air as you open the carriage window just after dawn for a first glimpse of Scotland (though it could scarcely seem other than sweet after the all-night fug of the train, or the fog back in Sheffield!). Or maybe the ticket-inspector on the overnight from Inverness as he sings out 'Change at Pairth' to every living soul on the train, as if delivering a sacrament, the voice approaching and receding along the train and heard against the rhythm of a 'Black Five' (or was it two engines?) slogging and hooting away in front: music has been fashioned from such ingredients! (Steve Reich's *Different Trains* for example.) And, as to creature comforts, not many railway enthusiasts visiting Glasgow in the 1950s will have failed to sample, at least once, the spartan hospitality of the YMCA in Bothwell Street, with its slamming doors, stern janitors and aroma of porridge; a few may have contrasted it with the more plush hotel on Edinburgh's North Bridge, high above the Waverley, where all night long your dreams were infused with the chime whistles of 'A4s', invisible in the vast station below.

I could go on in this vein of personal reminiscence, and probably shall (hopefully, not *too* tiresomely) in the picture captions — about which I should add a word of caution. As an 'armchair researcher', my sources are often second- or third-hand, so those in search of historical facts should perhaps not trust me, and look elsewhere; even so, the books and periodicals that have provided information are many and varied, and rather too numerous to list. However, it is the pictures that are nine-tenths of the book and, although one cannot now say with the same certainty as of old that 'the camera cannot lie', I can at least vouch for their authenticity!

This preamble began in a camera shop so, for a final piquancy of Scotland in the 1960s, let me end in another. Picture this one in a quiet street in Perth. Nothing much in the window except a few dusty Kodak boxes, but it holds the promise of what you are seeking. No longer the box-camera tyro, you go in and ask for film: Tri X Professional. 'Eh, Tri X y'say?' The proprietor at first sounds a little uninterested, but reiteration of the word (and I blush now for the conceit of it!) 'professional' suddenly switches the lights on in his tired, old eyes. Now avid, he lowers his voice conspiratorially, even though there's nobody else in the shop: 'So! There has been a sighting, then?' Of what?, you wonder. 'Ah, come on now, you can tell me — in the strictest confidence, of course.' What's he on about? After more cajolery, still cloaked in mystery, he finally gets a bit stroppy: 'Now look here boys, come off it! Don't tell me you're *not* up for The Monster!'

For heaven's sake, don't. Or you will find your film, professional, regular, or substitute, is firmly out of stock!

Derek Penney
March 1999

'The road goes ever on...' from Rannoch, West Highland line, in June 1960. Class 'K4' locomotive No 61995 *Cameron of Lochiel*.

Left: In 1958 a journey to Scotland took me by way of the 'Waverley' route from Carlisle to Edinburgh. This had been built originally to serve the cloth manufacturing towns along the Tweed and its tributaries, and of which Hawick was to become the principal staging point on the line. Pausing there on a cold August morning — one of those when early brightness is quickly snuffed out — is one of the many express good trains that were a feature of traffic on this steeply-graded line. Whitrope summit has been conquered but, with the climb to Falahill further ahead, it's as well that Class V2 No 60883 has a good head of steam. The Gresley 2-6-2s virtually monopolised these workings for many years, before being joined by Pacifics displaced from passenger duties during the transition to diesel power.

Above: The railway was carried high above the grey mill town of Hawick on a curving viaduct from which the narrow, wooden-boarded station platforms were cantilevered out. This 1958 view of Class B1 4-6-0 No 61308 on an Edinburgh to Carlisle stopping train shows why the signal cabin (seen more prominently in the photograph opposite) had to be perched so high to give the signalman a clear sight of the station. The line from Edinburgh to Hawick had opened in 1849, and onwards to Carlisle in 1862, but it did not prosper until completion of the Midland Railway's Settle to Carlisle line in 1876. Even then the line was never to be a good earner and its future was in jeopardy just 10 years after these photographs were taken. It finally closed on 6 January 1969.

Not quite as frantic as it must have been in its heyday, when there were almost as many trains moving in or out of its 19 platforms as there were minutes in the day, the Waverley station in Edinburgh was still one of the largest and busiest in the country when photographed from the west end on an August afternoon in 1958. Dominating the skyline on the left is the North British Hotel, from which the North Bridge vaults across the station to the Carlton Hotel opposite. There I would later lie, sleepless, marvelling at how many 'A4s' used the station at dead of night. But the mellifluous sounds I was to hear did not include the uniquely deep-toned hooter of No 60013 *Dominion of New Zealand*, lately arrived with the 'Elizabethan' and having to work overtime remarshalling the train, her 6½hr nonstop run from King's Cross notwithstanding.

Caught in an idle moment at her makeshift depot at the opposite end of Waverley station is one of the selected members of Class 'J83' that acted as station pilots here. In common with some other large stations at this time, Waverley was fortunate in having exceptional care lavished on its pilots and, although not the pre-Grouping livery sported at places such as York and Liverpool Street, No 68470's plain black paintwork could not have been more lovingly maintained. Designed by Matthew Holmes, 40 of these 45-ton locomotives were built for the NBR at the turn of the century, and most survived to pass into BR ownership. The stronghold forming the background is the Calton Hill jail; the aspect of its windows prompts the thought that occupancy of 'a cell with a view' might have made it one of the least disagreeable places in which to be incarcerated — although I would not argue the point with anyone!

Above: From one of the grandest of Scottish stations my path took me a few days later to one of the most diminutive — Killin, on the branch from the Callander & Oban line. Opened in 1886 as the Killin Railway Company, it began its existence as a private local concern headed by the Marquis of Breadalbane. It was worked, but never owned, by the Caledonian, and at the Grouping it was acquired by the LMS directly from the estate of the recently deceased Marquis. One of the ex-Caledonian engines still employed on the line in September 1958, No 55222 of the McIntosh '439' class, is shown here shunting the tiny yard after leaving her train at the single platform (behind the camera position). As there was no passing loop here, I was mystified as to how the locomotive would get round its train: 'Ah well, that's something for you to be thinking about' teased the driver.

Right: The line originally terminated alongside the shore of Loch Tay, where the trains connected with steamers. When these were withdrawn in 1939, so was the train service between Killin and Loch Tay, although the line itself was kept open to allow the branch engine to be stabled and serviced at the small wooden shed situated at the very end of the line. I accepted with gusto an invitation to accompany the crew there on the midday trip — footplate rides were easier to come by the further away from 'head office' you were! — and duly photographed the engine there in her idyllic arbour. In common with the Waverley were the wagons serving as a coaling stage; they occupy the now-redundant run-round loop.

Below: Siesta time for No 55222 and her crew meant time to kill for me. After again photographing the locomotive, now repositioned in another sylvan setting, a period of rather dispiriting inactivity ensued and I was glad when the time came to depart back to Killin. There I learned how the engine was manoeuvred to the front of the train: by its being placed in the siding while the guard 'drove' the train past simply by releasing its handbrake and allowing it to trundle down the gradient until clear of the points. So simple, but I hadn't worked it out!

Right: Backed by the superb mountain scenery, Ben Lawers prominent, No 55222 is shown departing from Killin with the early afternoon train. It was uphill all the way to the Junction for the veteran locomotive and she seems to be struggling a little, even on this fine afternoon. You could not imagine the huge BR standard Class 4 2-6-4Ts which later supplanted these 'Caley' 0-4-4Ts being troubled by any combination of wet leaves or 'the wrong kind of snow' with their usual one-coach train! With closure planned for 1 November 1965, along with the Oban line as far as Crianlarich, the branch came to a premature end when a landslide blocked the main line at Glenogle, the last train leaving Killin on 27 September.

Above: The Company tradition of using 4-4-0 locomotives for both passenger and goods work ensured that the type outnumbered all others by around five to one on the former Great North of Scotland Railway. Built in 1920 by the North British Locomotive Co, No 49 *Gordon Highlander*, of the final superheated Class F, was the last of them to remain in BR service when withdrawn in June 1958. It was then repainted as depicted here and put into occasional service by the Scottish Region on railtours and promotional specials. One of these, the SLS 'Golden Jubilee Special', had in June 1959 taken the locomotive to Dumfries in the territory of the former Glasgow & South Western Railway — the very opposite corner of the country to its natural habitat. Although it was the 13th of the month, the day was lucky for the youthful pleasure riders (not joyriders!) as the engine leaves the motive power depot.

Right: Gordon Highlander had arrived in Dumfries by way of the Caledonian Railway's branch from Lockerbie, the venture that had allowed that company to seize, and retain for many years, control of the Portpatrick & Wigtownshire Railway, deep in G&SW territory. Ironically, that 'Caley' presence was still evident in the motive power on view in the shed yard that day. Nearest the camera is 0-6-0 standard goods, or 'Jumbo', No 57302, the design of which was originated by Dugald Drummond; beyond it is No 57623, a McIntosh '812' class and essentially a larger version of the 'Jumbo'. Both had outlasted all their G&SW rivals by many years.

Below: Dumfries was an important junction, particularly for services from the south, for it was here that the line to Stranraer via the aforementioned P&WR, the so-called 'Port Road', branched westward from the G&SW Carlisle to Glasgow main line. This scene has a 'rush hour' appearance as Leeds-based 'Royal Scot' 4-6-0 No 46113 *Cameronian* restarts the down Thames-Clyde Express, while back in the station a BR standard Class 4 2-6-4T and *Gordon Highlander* are preparing for departure. On the far right an ex-LMS standard '2P' 4-4-0, with empty stock for another service, waits its turn for a platform.

Right: On the return journey to Glasgow *Gordon Highlander* was booked to run nonstop from Dumfries to Kilmarnock, but the heavy climb to New Cumnock rather took the 'Old Soldier's' breath away and there was an enforced stop to recuperate. Given the time of day and position of the sun you might well surmise the train to be southbound (it had me reaching for the map); here the line runs due west, but the approaching solstice has allowed the setting sun to steal around to the northern side of the line.

Left: The Gresley 'V1' express tank design of 1930 was particularly associated with ex-LNER lines in Scotland, which were allocated around two-thirds of the class of 92 locomotives. They followed the customary Gresley principle of having the middle axle driven by all three cylinders, of which the inside one was steeply inclined to allow the connecting rod to clear the leading coupled axle. The final 10 engines were classified 'V3' by virtue of having increased boiler pressure, and many 'V1s' were similarly converted during the postwar years. I could never discern any difference in outward appearance between 'V1s' and 'V3s', although there were variations within both classes. The original engines had elbowed steam pipes; others sported straight ones such as are seen on 'V1' No 67664, ex-works at Eastfield shed; and engines built from 1935 onwards had built-up coal bunkers instead of the coal-railed type originally provided.

This page: Typical of the duties these 2-6-2Ts performed was haulage of local trains on the north bank of the Clyde, part of Glasgow's cross-city suburban services to such destinations as Helensburgh, and Balloch where these views show 'V3s' No 67607 (below) arriving and No 67611 (above) awaiting departure. The day was glorious and the trains packed with trippers to Loch Lomond. One of the drivers bore a resemblance to the actor John Laurie and was very much a 'Private Fraser' before his time (*Dad's Army* was yet to come). Lamenting having to work on such a day, he rolled his eyes to the flawless blue sky, intoning: 'Phenom'nal! Qui-te phenom'nal!' Then, eyeballing me with a Fraser-like glare: 'But it may *not* last!' — a thought not absent from my own mind. If I had asked him what he thought of 'V3s' he might well have said: 'They're rubbish man — ahm tellin ye straight!'

Above: The fine weather did last a little while, but two days later, to escape persistent torrential rain, I foolishly entered a Glasgow cinema. Not for the first time was I punished for such dereliction of duty by stumbling out two hours later into blinding sunlight: would I ever learn? Hastening to Central station, all I could muster was this snapshot of No 46229 *Duchess of Hamilton* arriving with the down 'Royal Scot'.

Right: That 'phenomenal' day had been the start of a holiday the main focus of interest of which was on the activities of the last two 'C15' 4-4-2Ts — those 'Yorkshire tanks' alluded to in the Introduction — and the County Donegal Railway across the water. And so, next day, to Eastfield where surprisingly, and almost as if by prior arrangement, No 67460 was outside the shed in splendid isolation. Part of a class of 30 locomotives, designed by W. P. Reid and built for the NBR by the Yorkshire Engine Company (maker's number 1073 of 1912), her origin prompts the thought that Glasgow's mighty locomotive industry must have had an abundance of business to have allowed such a substantial order to slip away to one of the 'minnows' of the trade. This engine's presence here meant that the other survivor, No 67474, would be in service on the West Highland line the following day.

Left: Here is No 67474 taking water at Garelochhead while working the Craigendoran to Arrochar push-and-pull train on 15 June 1959. The road ahead is already clear for departure of this northbound train, of which this is a rear view. Only the fireman will remain on the footplate, the driver controlling both brakes and the locomotive's vacuum-operated regulator from the driving compartment at the opposite end of the train. Although a jaunt on the engine would have been even more welcome, I had to consider myself lucky to be invited to ride with the driver — where I could be under his eyes, not the fireman's feet, I suppose!

Above: From Garelochhead the line rises steeply to 564ft above sea level at Glen Douglas, a summit reached in the opposite direction by an equally fierce climb from Arrochar & Tarbet, situated on the low-lying isthmus between Loch Long and Loch Lomond. With the 1 in 57 gradient facing them, Class 5 4-6-0 No 44957 and 'K2' 2-6-0 No 61787 *Loch Quoich* restart a southbound train from Arrochar & Tarbet station. The 'K2s' had enjoyed many years of successful service on the West Highland but were nearing the end of their days; this one would be the 'assisting' engine and, conforming with a practice dating back to NBR days, is positioned behind the 'train' engine.

Below: It was pleasing to see No 67474 in the spruce condition she displays here during a relaxed interlude at Arrochar & Tarbet station, of which the chalet-like building, set on an island platform, was characteristic of many on this line. My only mode of transport was the train, and its midday sojourn here tempted me to risk going on foot to the next station to photograph the train arriving. Later, on that baking-hot day, it seemed a reckless decision as I found myself stranded on the road, far below the line, with not-too-distant whistles sounding. But my despair had been noticed: 'If it's the train you're wanting, hop on' — a stout gentleman on a moped that seemed scarcely able to carry him had stopped alongside me. He inched forward to provide an impossibly small pillion. I doubted. He insisted. The ride that ensued was more heart-stopping than any fairground could have provided, as the gallant little machine, weaving from side to side of the narrow road to beat the gradient, carried its owner, myself and all my

impedimenta up the mountainside to Glen Douglas station. Happening so quickly, the episode was little short of the surreal, needing perhaps only 'The Ride of the Valkyries' as accompaniment to make it totally so! Yet that spontaneous and unlooked-for act of kindness enabled me to secure the shot that appears on the cover; and although my saviour would not have known that a mere photograph was all that was at stake, the credit for it should certainly be his.

Right: Situated at the head of the glen and high above Loch Long, the station called Glen Douglas was simply a passing loop with a signal cabin and, when the railway was dormant, a place of profound quiet. Disturbing the calm after the storm of my undignified arrival there, BR standard Class 5 No 73078 passes with an up express.

Left: Another Class 5, No 44968, one of the more familiar Stanier 4-6-0s which were then predominant on the West Highland motive power scene, begins the steep descent to Arrochar & Tarbet with a train bound for Fort William. Glen Douglas signal cabin is just visible above the end of the train.

Below: Apart from the 'assisting' 'K2' pictured earlier, no ex-LNER engines were seen in operation on the through services that day, but on a visit to the line a year earlier 'B1s' were more in evidence. This one, No 61340 of Eastfield shed, is arriving at Crianlarich. However, 'K2s' and the later Peppercorn 'K1' 2-6-0s still held sway on the line from Fort William to Mallaig, where the turntable could not, at that time, accommodate 4-6-0s.

Above: Graffiti then being more discreet than today, the baffled or intrigued rail traveller in the 1950s might just discern on the wall of some waiting room in central England a carefully pencilled message to the effect that its writer had 'died here waiting for *Cicero*'. This cry from the heart held meaning only for those who had known the peculiar longing it conveyed. For No 60101 was one of the select band of 'A3s' whose working lives were spent entirely on Scottish lines, and whose appearances south of Tyne or Solway were few and far between. The canny 'spotter' could, however, avoid this kind of despair by relying on intelligence from friendly Doncaster apprentices as to when the sorely wanted one was undergoing overhaul in the 'Plant' (output of which would then be patiently monitored). By this tactic many such rarities would fall into the net without ever setting foot over the Border. The only risk to life or limb would come from shinning up lamp posts to glimpse *Blenheim*, or some other, in the paint shop. Enough! *Cicero*, photographed when such monkey business was history, is on the turntable at Haymarket shed, Edinburgh, in August 1958.

Right: Moving off Haymarket the following year is the Caledonian Railway 4-2-2 No 123. Of the four restored Scottish pre-Grouping locomotives operating at that time, this is perhaps the most renowned. Displayed at the Edinburgh Exhibition of 1885, the engine had been designed and built by Neilsen and Co, though it was similar in outline and detail to the Drummond 4-4-0s of this time. Although her type was not perpetuated by the great man, she secured enduring fame in the 1888 London to Edinburgh 'races' between the East and West Coast routes, when she was the regular engine from Carlisle to Edinburgh. No 123 remained in the limelight in the early 1900s when designated the official inspection engine and 'Royal Pilot' of the CR, and was withdrawn from LMS service in 1935.

Above: On 13 June 1960, a special train bound for Macduff departed from the original 1856 Aberdeen Waterloo terminus, closed to passenger traffic as long ago as 1867 when the 'Joint' station was opened. Much was made of the retrospective event, the *Railway Observer* declaring it as being 'beyond the ken of any local sage', although I recall being less than overwhelmed by the experience. Far more stirring for me was the sight of *Gordon Highlander*, newly-repainted in a richer shade of green than that seen on my last encounter with the locomotive exactly one year earlier.

Right: The journey to Macduff was part of a week-long railtour, organised jointly by the RCTS and SLS, visiting lines little used or threatened with closure. A lengthy stop at Inverurie allowed a visit to the ex-GNSR works where, in the graveyard of condemned locomotives, were seen the last of Classes Z4 and Z5, those GNSR 0-4-2Ts which had long been a familiar sight on Aberdeen quaysides. It was more heartening to see such a venerable machine as ex-NBR 0-6-0 No 65265 (*above*), of Class J36, newly outshopped and repainted. Another refurbished NBR 0-6-0 undergoing steaming trials was 'J37' No 64635 (*below*).

Left: Leaving the main line to Keith at Inveramsay, the railtour train paused at Turriff, the principal intermediate station on the Macduff branch. In contrast to Waterloo terminus this was recognisably a station, and an amazingly well-preserved one as well, considering that the passenger service on the branch had ceased on 1 October 1951. Without doubt, the well-enclosed platforms would have provided welcome shelter when raw winter winds were scything across this exposed region. Turriff remained open for freight traffic until 3 January 1966.

Below: It took 2hr to cover the 30 rambling miles from Inveramsay before *Gordon Highlander* arrived at the spectacular clifftop terminus at Macduff. Sturdily built of stone and overall-roofed as it needed to be — even the June wind had an edge — the station is unfortunately obscured in this view by steam from the locomotive now moving to the head of the train after having made use of the turntable just off to the right of the scene. Engines of this 'D40' and the older 'D41' classes would have handled the four or so daily through services from Aberdeen which the branch enjoyed in prewar days. At this time, only a daily freight operated, usually worked by a 'J36', and this would cease when the line from Turriff was closed on 1 August 1961.

Nowadays 'Industrial Designers' are employed to create 'style' and ensure that engineering products appeal to the eyes of consumers. The ever-changing liveries of present-day 'HSTs' also bear witness to their efforts, while back in steam days perhaps the Gresley 'A4s' were the first locomotives to display self-conscious 'industrial design'. But my point is that before that profession emerged, engineers themselves were expected to be their own stylists and machines such as this are surely proof that their work required no improvement. *Gordon Highlander*, photographed at Kintore on 13 June 1960, now resides permanently in the Glasgow Museum of Transport.

Given that *Gordon Highlander's* immaculate turn-out was to be expected, perhaps even more praiseworthy was the cleanliness of these two workaday engines pictured at Elgin, although one suspects that for Class 5 No 45476, of Inverness shed, this will be but a short-lived flowering of 'ex-works' paintwork. In full forward gear, she is ready for blast-off with a short local train while ex-LMS Class 2P No 40663, either the object of tender loving care or forced labour, waits demurely for her turn of duty.

Above: The railway had reached Forres from Inverness in 1858 and was extended to Keith later in the year, thus completing the link with Aberdeen which survives today. Three years later, amid spectacular local pageantry, the first sod was cut of the future Highland Railway main line — to Perth, over Dava Moor — seen in the right foreground of this view. There was entertainment on this 1960 day also, but intended less for the locals than the passengers on this special train as it was manoeuvred around all three sides of the triangular junction at Forres, thus leaving the locomotive the wrong way round and having to do another circuit! With all this palaver over, '2P' 4-4-0 No 40663 is ready for departure to Inverness. The line over Dava Moor was abandoned in the mid-1960s in favour of the later and more direct route from Inverness to Aviemore, via Carrbridge.

Right: Later on that day of 14 June, the dazzling sunshine of Forres gave way to leaden skies for what was the most immediately valedictory event of the week: the last train ever, passenger or freight, on the line from Muir of Ord to Fortrose. Ex-CR 0-6-0 No 57594, the locomotive entrusted with the task of hauling it, was scarcely up to the job and her progress was marked with anxiety on the 1 in 60 banks that abounded on the line. This view shows the returning train at Munlochy, where the drizzling rain did not deter local folk from turning out to witness the mournful event. Dubbed 'the Black Isle line', this former HR branch of 1894 took its name from the peninsula, between the Firths of Cromarty and Inverness, that it served.

Below: Awaiting the passing of a down freight at Aviemore, that respite from gradients to the north and to the south, is 'Jones Goods' No 103 of 1894. The earliest of 15 engines built by Sharp, Stewart & Co at the Atlas works in Glasgow, and famed as the first 4-6-0 to operate in Britain, she had been withdrawn from regular service in 1934 and kept at St Rollox works. It was there — painted as I recall in a more greenish shade of yellow than displayed here — that I first encountered the locomotive almost a decade earlier, when it would have been in the realms of fantasy to imagine making a journey behind her on her own turf, the Highland main line.

Right: Although the credit for the design of No 103 goes to HR locomotive superintendent David Jones, it has been persuasively argued that, despite cosmetic Highland features, this owes less to his previous work for the company than to the long series of 4-6-0s produced by Glasgow firms from 1880 onwards for service in India and elsewhere overseas. It would not have been the first, nor the last, time that a main line railway had entrusted design work to a contractor: one thinks of the LNER 'Sandringhams' and LMS 'Royal Scots', and then back to the CR 'Single' No 123. Here, having breasted the highest main line summit in Britain, 1,484ft above sea level in the Pass of Drumochty, No 103 has an unexpectedly long sojourn at Blair Atholl. Despite the engine's heroic efforts, evidenced by the burnt paintwork on the smokebox, we had fallen so far behind schedule that the special's path, ahead of a Perth local, had been lost — not a misfortune for me as it allowed plenty of time for the sun to come out.

Above: The last of a long line of Caledonian Railway 4-4-0 types was the Pickersgill '72' class of 1920. It rounded off a tradition which had begun with Dugald Drummond's '66' class of 1884-5 and continued, with a gradual increment of size, in designs by each of his successors — most notably the famous 'Dunalastair' series of J. F. McIntosh. Perth's No 54485 had been smartened up for duty on the special train seen here at the north end of the station. An added touch of nostalgia was provided by the two restored Caledonian carriages, fortuitously marshalled at the front of the train, leaving only the locomotive's one-time sky-blue livery to the imagination.

Right: It was the task of No 54485 to haul the special train 'at a speed not to exceed 20mph' to Crieff and Comrie by way of the goods-only Almond Valley line. She is seen here at Ruthven Road soon after taking to this quiet byway at Almond Valley Junction, just north of Perth. Passenger services had ceased in 1951, at which time a westward extension to Balquhidder on the Callander & Oban line had closed entirely. Crieff continued to enjoy a passenger service from Gleneagles and it was via that route that the train returned to Perth, allowing the 4-4-0 to be let off the leash on the descent of Strath Earn.

Opened in 1854, the sole purpose of the line from Elliot Junction, on the Dundee & Arbroath Railway, to Carmyllie was to carry stone and slate from the extensive quarries thereabouts. A passenger service was introduced in 1900, by which time the line had become a public railway worked by the CR and NBR in alternate years. Two ex-LMS Ivatt Class 2MT 2-6-0s were needed to haul this five-coach special up the steeply-graded line. These having arrived at Carmyllie chimney-to-chimney, No 46464 has already been detached and drawn forward leaving only No 46463 at the head of the train as it stands at the tiny station: just the start of a complicated manoeuvre to get both locomotives to the other end of the train tender-to-tender. The passenger service had been withdrawn in 1929, but the line did not finally close until 24 May 1965, almost five years after this photograph was taken.

In comparison to Carmyllie, the station layout at Kirriemuir has the appearance of a major terminus yet it, too, was without a regular passenger service and would close altogether even earlier, on 21 January 1965. The locomotive is one of the time-honoured Drummond 'Jumbo' standard goods 0-6-0s: No 57441. One wonders, but perhaps fears to discover, what in the name of progress has now replaced this charming scene.

Below: Despite having had no passenger service for the past five years the station at Newburgh, on the southern side of the Firth of Tay, still looks spruce and serviceable as ex-NBR 4-4-0 No 256 *Glen Douglas* arrives from Perth. This station is on the section of line, from Ladybank to Hilton Junction, that had been part of the original Edinburgh to Perth route before the more direct line via Cowdenbeath and Glenfarg was opened. Of secondary importance in 1960, it was destined to again carry Edinburgh to Perth traffic when the direct line was closed in 1975.

Right: Glen Douglas, withdrawn from regular service in 1959 as Class D34 No 62469, was another of the quartet of locomotives restored to 'pre-Grouping' condition by BR's Scottish Region, her hard-to-describe NBR livery thought by those familiar with it to have been extremely well captured. Here she stands at another well-maintained station: Auchtermuchty, on the freight-only line from Ladybank which was to close in 1964. It made connection with the Edinburgh to Perth line at Mawcarse Junction, to where the train is awaiting departure.

Above: The 'White Cockade' railtour train is shown on arrival at Fort William on 18 June 1960. The inclement weather that marred much of the journey from Glasgow is only just beginning to lift as the station pilot, a 'J36' 0-6-0, attaches to the carriages to release the train engine, ex-LNER Class K4 2-6-0 No 61995 *Cameron of Lochiel*. The small waterfront station beside Loch Linnhe is the hub of the West Highland Railway and terminus for trains from both Glasgow and Mallaig directions.

Right: The engine shed, built close to the site of the military fort which had given the town of Fort William its name, was still a stronghold of steam power, although the ex-LMS 'Black Fives' which had by then come to dominate workings on the West Highland line are not much in evidence in this view. *Cameron of Lochiel* receives attention on the right, while a 'J36' 0-6-0 has manoeuvred on to the turntable an observation car used on the Mallaig line. This vehicle, originally used on the prewar 'Coronation' express, has had its streamlined 'beaver-tail' remodelled.

Below: The six locomotives of LNER Class K4 were introduced in 1937 specifically to suit the arduous conditions on the West Highland line. With 5ft 2in driving wheels and three cylinders, compared to the 5ft 8in and two cylinders of the 'K2s' hitherto used, they were able to increase the maximum unassisted train load from 220 tons to 300 tons; and their economical use of water required them to replenish the tender only once between Fort William and Glasgow. That would be at Crianlarich, a place also renowned for its refreshment facilities for hungry and thirsty travellers since the days before these came to be provided on the trains, and where *Cameron of Lochiel* pauses on the return journey from Fort William. With its island platform layout and chalet-style buildings the station exemplified many on the line, but on a scale befitting its importance. The expectation that this would be the last appearance ever on the West Highland of one of these engines, then eking out a lowly existence in faraway Fife, was happily proved false.

Right: Crianlarich was where the West Highland crossed over and connected, via a little-used spur, with the Callander & Oban line along which 'The White Cockade' was to continue to Glasgow, occasioning perhaps the first ever visit of a 'K4' to that line. Awaiting crossing with a down train, No 61995 is pictured at Killin Junction in late evening sunshine: a view which shows the odd, elbowed steam pipe carried on the left-hand side of the engine. Steam rises from the Killin branch train, out of sight on the adjacent platform but still powered by a 'Caley' 0-4-4T, No 55173, almost a year on from my last visit. This section of the Callander & Oban is now abandoned, its traffic using the West Highland to Crianlarich, thence via the aforementioned spur to Oban.

A year or so after being restored to LNER livery, No 4472 *Flying Scotsman* was portrayed on the Forth Bridge by railway artist Cuneo. In between 'sittings' for the work she would repair to Inverkeithing, near to where she is here depicted on one of those movements. Later that week the locomotive was used on a local railtour, and it was whilst awaiting this near Milnathort that a companion and I were accosted by a gentleman of lordly bearing, but shabby raiment, crying: 'Sassenachs! Sassenachs, I'll be bound!' Having caused maximum consternation — it seemed more than possible it was his field we were standing in! — he grinned and affably enquired: 'And whereabouts in England *are* you from boys?' 'Sheffield! Och, that noo really England!' Then he cast his line again. Leaning his chin on the wooden fence post and surveying the line he murmured, oh so casually: 'And I suppose you've come to see *our* "Scotsman".' Our instant protests were cut short by a wink and a wagging, 'got-you-again' finger. With more teasing to come, the company of this genial man lifted the gloom of unkind weather and a belated appearance by the famous engine.

Twenty of the BR standard Class 5 4-6-0s were turned out with Caprotti valve gear, of which 10 were at one time allocated to St Rollox shed. One of these was No 73150 which, although not fully repainted, has clearly been recently outshopped following attention to its cylinders and valves. The locomotive is making ready to leave Perth with the 5.30pm Buchanan Street to Aberdeen, one of the 3hr expresses usually enjoying Pacific-haulage that, if needs must, could be capably handled by a 4-6-0 in good form.

Above: Remembering the LNER 'B1' 4-6-0s from the immediate postwar years when they were the latest and greatest, in smart green livery while all else was still dowdy and 'NE', their 'mixed-traffic' designation would rarely extend to using them on loose-coupled coal trains. That heyday was long gone by 1964 when dieselisation of so many passenger services meant that, for Thornton Junction's 'B1s', such plebeian duties had become commonplace. No 61118, passing Perth motive power depot, is fortunately clean enough to show the distinctive touch seemingly bestowed only on Scottish 'B1s' shopped at Cowlairs Works, whereby the running plate valance was filled out in the corners to provide a flowing contour, an effect emphasised by the lining-out.

Right: The coal traffic through Perth would have been usual forage for such engines as the LNER 'J38' 0-6-0s, another of those Gresley types built for service exclusively in Scotland. Much of the former NBR's coalfield network in Fife and the Lothians was barred to eight-coupled goods engines, but the 'J38s' were a powerful alternative, being the only ex-LNER 0-6-0s to receive the BR '6F' classification. The very similar, but larger-wheeled, 'J39s', also introduced in 1926, went on to number 289 locomotives, but when they became extinct in December 1962, 30 out of 35 'J38s' still survived, including No 65929, which is seen leaving Perth shed. A 'plain Jane' of an engine, maybe, but those on the footplate seem quite happy to be seen with her!

Left: In prewar days the journey time between Glasgow and Aberdeen had been cut to 3hr by the best LMS expresses. This rapidity of travel was not restored until 1962 when, following successful trial runs by 'A4' No 60027 *Merlin*, ex-LNER Pacifics were introduced on to this former LMS trunk route. With only moderate loads the 3hr timing was well within the capabilities of the Pacifics, whose four-year reign became one of the splendours of the Scottish railway scene during the rundown of steam. One of the ex-Haymarket 'A4s' then shedded at Ferryhill, No 60009 *Union of South Africa* is getting away from Perth with the 5.30pm Glasgow to Aberdeen, formerly known as the 'Saint Mungo'.

Below: The influx of Pacifics was such that at one point Ferryhill had no fewer than 10 'A4s' on its books, so it is not surprising that the engines were found work on other than the prestigious Aberdeen to Glasgow expresses. One such regular duty was working the Aberdeen portion of the 'West Coast Postal' southwards from Perth, which on this May 1964 day is entrusted to English *émigré* No 60016 *Silver King*. This concentration of 'A4' power became a magnet for enthusiasts from all parts, and Perth, as may be gathered from the photographs that follow, was at that time one of the liveliest steam centres in Scotland and an ideal base of operations.

Left: The afternoon fish train from Aberdeen to the south changed engines at Perth, being usually taken forward by a Carlisle-based steam locomotive. On this occasion it was BR standard Pacific No 70038 *Robin Hood*, whose name reminds me that this 'Britannia' was once stationed at March, in the far away fenlands, from where its forays up the GN & GE 'Joint' line would have taken it through territory more associated with its namesake. I have sometimes wondered — but, mind you, this is not a complaint! — why the 'Britannias' were not used on the '3hr' trains, for which they might have been a more expected choice than the 'A4s'. They would undoubtedly have done well, as would the ex-LMS Pacifics which were also extant at the time.

Above: As Nationalisation approached, a number of 'B1s' were hastily given the names of directors of the LNER Company. (What an escape for *Golden Eagle*, *Kingfisher*, et al — even *Mallard* might not have been safe!) Among the curious mixture a few sounded well, none more so than *Murray of Elibank* which might have passed muster on a 'K4'. Here, No 61221 *Sir Alexander Erskine-Hill* (miniature lettering on the nameplate to get it all in) is leaving Perth on a mixed freight in May 1964 and displays its home depot 'Haymarket' painted on the buffer beam, an LNER custom still continued at the time at Cowlairs Works. In contradiction, its smokebox shed plate indicates that the engine belongs to Thornton Junction!

Left: Few journeys could be undertaken on Scottish lines without encountering the Stanier 'Black Five' 4-6-0s. Arguably, if you discount sheer weight of numbers, they had proved themselves ideal 'all-rounders' for Scottish conditions, so widespread had their use become in the 1960s. This angle of view clearly shows the domeless taper boiler, that feature of GWR practice their Swindon-trained designer brought with him to the LMS, which was provided on early examples of the class. Once a Perth engine, at this time of Carstairs, No 45011 is here revisiting her former home and is sporting a repaint that has omitted the lining below the running plate.

Below: I've heard it said more than once (and very dogmatically, of course!) that if there's anything better than a 'Black Five', it's two! Even the Perth signalbox supervisor expressed a similar sentiment on the day of this photograph. From personal experience on the Midland main line, the combination was almost a guarantee of lively running; but this was Scotland and a brace of 'black'uns' at Perth perhaps intimates some mighty task of haulage on the Highland main line. Actually, Nos 44961 and 44925 were waiting to take the Aberdeen 'Fish' forward to Carlisle, a task that was often entrusted to a single locomotive of Class 7 power.

Left: More than a year has passed and I'm again at Perth photographing a southbound parcels train in the cutting leading to Moncrieff tunnel. The nameplates have already been removed from 'Britannia' 4-6-2 No 70008 *Hotspur* and the locomotive's deplorable state of external care was indicative of the neglect of steam, already commonplace in some quarters, which was to become more widespread as dieselisation progressed.

Below: Not quite as unkempt as the 'Britannia' is this 'Black Five', pictured later in the day at the same spot. This was one of the later batches of the class which had the boiler top feed positioned further forward. It's odd how such small changes in outline can so alter, for good or ill, the appearance of a locomotive. A novel feature that did not affect the external appearance was the steel firebox that 10 of the class, including No 44727, were built with.

At the end of August 1965, ex-LNER 'A2' Pacific No 60530 *Sayajirao* was given a rare outing on the 10.00am Dundee to Glasgow express, returning on the 6.15pm from Buchanan Street. A second appearance the following day probably surprised even the authorities at Dundee, who resolutely prevented the hat-trick by turning out the dirtiest Class 5 in the world on the third morning. This was in the twilight days of the three remaining 'A2s', so, as word got around, cameras popped up all over the place to record the unexpected treat, much to the chagrin of its instigator who had been expecting a 'scoop'. The train is seen at Hilton Junction on 1 September, with the ex-NBR line to Fife and Edinburgh in the foreground.

Heading back to Fife over the eastward fork at Hilton Junction is Class WD 2-8-0 No 90041 with a short train of coal empties. The junction lies just south of Moncrieff tunnel which in its early years was the cause of bitter wrangles between its owners, the Scottish Central (later Caledonian) Railway, and the Edinburgh, Newburgh & Perth Railway over the payment of tolls. At the height of the dispute, with the EN&P refusing to pay, its trains were held up somewhere hereabouts while the dues were extracted from individual passengers. Enough, one would think, to provoke a modicum of 'rail-rage' — and it probably did!

Left: Trains southbound from Perth have an easy run for the first few miles up Strath Earn until they encounter a seven-mile climb, the last four at 1 in 100, to a summit half a mile beyond Gleneagles station, the platform of which is seen beyond the overbridge. This meant a taxing start for trains stopping there — although I doubt whether this one had, so well into her stride seems 'Black Five' No 44997. The missing semaphores on the signal bracket indicate that the line to Crieff was already closed at the time of this view in September 1965. Originally Crieff Junction, the station name was changed to concur with that of the nearby complex of golf courses and the deluxe hotel, the construction of which was started by the Caledonian but not completed by the LMS until 1924.

Above: The last 'A4' to be built, and one of only four to carry the Kylchap double blast pipe and chimney from the start, was LNER No 4903 *Peregrine*. Renamed *Lord Faringdon* in 1948, following withdrawal of the ex-Great Central 4-6-0 which had hitherto carried the name of the former GCR and LNER Director, the locomotive already had to her credit 25 years of service on the GN main line when transferred to Scotland in October 1963. After winter storage at Galashiels and Bathgate, No 60034 was in May 1964 put to work on the Glasgow to Aberdeen run, on which she was still employed a year or so later when seen crossing the Allan Water, north of Dunblane.

Left: Whereas *Lord Faringdon* appeared to be making light of the climb to Kinbuck, in a nearby location Caprotti-fitted BR Standard Class 5 No 73151 is clearly in travail. This 5½ miles of Dunblane bank, much of it at 1 in 88, is the northbound counterpart of the climb to Gleneagles, although the going gets easier beyond Kinbuck.

Below: Travelling in the opposite direction, 'A4' No 60024 *Kingfisher* eases away from Dunblane with the 1.30pm Aberdeen to Glasgow. This train, once known as the 'Grampian', was in May 1964 not one of the fastest. With a timing of 4hr it made more stops than the '3hr' trains, but they were often reached with time to spare.

Above: The centenary of the formation of the Highland Railway came about in 1965 and was marked in Inverness by a week of celebrations including the provision of a thrice-daily service to Forres and back, using the preserved 'Jones Goods' 4-6-0 and Caledonian carriages. The locomotive was to return to Perth and St Rollox workshops on 30 August, her last traversal of the Highland main line and the last by any steam-hauled train for many years to come. With the Black Isle across the water, she is seen here alongside Inverness Firth on the 2.40pm to Forres. This line was the Inverness & Nairn Railway of 1855, the first to serve the area.

Right: On 28 August 1965, when HR No 103 was making her last appearance on the Forres shuttle, NBR No 256 *Glen Douglas* hauled the RCTS 'Fife Coast Rail Tour', making a brave sight as she climbs the bank between Burntisland and Kinghorn. These veterans had not many more outings before being permanently installed in the Glasgow Museum of Transport, No 103 entering on 6 June 1966, followed three days later by No 256. The museum was not linked to the railway, necessitating removal of the locomotives by road, so it is likely they will never run again. But never say never!

Left: A clear September day in 1965 shows up the distant Sidlaw Hills across the Tay as Class 'J37' 0-6-0 No 64624 trundles, tender-first, off the bridge and away towards St Fort. Branching to the right beyond Wormit signal cabin is the loop line to Tayport, from where traffic to Dundee and the north would have been taken to the ferry in the days before the bridge was built (albeit arriving at Tayport in the opposite direction — from Leuchars, at the other end of the loop).

Below: That Tayport ferry would have tied up on the north bank at Broughty Ferry, near to where is seen this northbound express headed by 'Black Five' No 44703. It is passing over one of the oldest railways in Scotland, the Dundee & Arbroath, which was opened in 1838. Originally built to a gauge of 5ft 6in, it was soon to be converted to standard and in 1880 became a joint line between the Caledonian and the North British. The photograph was taken in August 1966.

Left: This location is but a few paces from the Drumlithie Hotel, in 1966 as hospitable an establishment as could be found anywhere. In fact, it was close enough to the inn to undertake the odyssey in pyjamas if the circumstance demanded, as well it might if you awakened to a morning as unexpectedly fine as this one and had the imminent prospect of an 'A4' on the 6.20am Aberdeen to Perth semi-fast. Unfortunately, the enterprise was not fully rewarded, but second prize was as pleasing a picture of a Stanier 'Black Five' as has ever come my way. Ah well, I'm away back to ma bed!

Above: We are now in the unforgettable summer of 1966. During the previous winter the 'A4' Pacifics had surrendered the '3hr' Glasgow-Aberdeen trains to diesel traction, but had been miraculously restored to working the 8.26am from Glasgow and 5.15pm return for the duration of the summer timetable. During the last week in June all three serviceable 'A4s' — Nos 60019, 60024 and 60034 – were active. Here, *Kingfisher* heads the 08.26 from Glasgow out of Stonehaven on 28th June.

Left: The 1.30pm 'Grampian' from Aberdeen is climbing away from the coastal town of Stonehaven behind 'A2' Pacific No 60532 *Blue Peter*, a new recruit to Ferryhill shed to bolster its dwindling number of 'A4s'. I reckon the nearest place on the map to this location is Fetteresso, away in the valley behind the locomotive; for the railway has now swung inland and threads its way into the hills by following the Carron Water to reach a summit at Carmont.

Below: Having topped the summit, 'A4' No 60034 *Lord Faringdon* is accelerating on the easier grade beyond it. Depicted again is the 1.30pm 'Grampian', and indicative of the winding nature of this section is the fact that the bearing of the train has been so altered that the sun now lights its opposite side. The date of this photograph is 29 June 1966, and it was to be the last time I saw this locomotive at work.

Below: 'Britannias' from Carlisle were still reaching Aberdeen on freight and special workings. Northbound from Stonehaven on 29 June 1966, No 70036 (once named *Boadicea*) was a welcome sight, despite the grime.

Right: Prospects could not have been bleaker on arrival at this lovely location, near Carmont, on a sombre afternoon as chilly and cheerless as June could offer; and there was an age to wait for the expected 'A4' on the 5.15pm up. Hearteningly, there soon appeared a small rift in the cloud sheet, and sunbeams slanted down to light this section of the line — and this alone — with theatrical precision. One's pulse might have quickened had a chime whistle just sounded somewhere around the curve, but that wasn't to be. The stroke of luck had come too soon, and it couldn't last. But last it did, as will be guessed, or I wouldn't be telling the tale! The 'Fish', the 'Postal', the 'Edinburgh' — all tantalisingly diesel-hauled — enjoyed the sun's localised blessing while all around remained dark. By the time *Kingfisher* finally appeared the issue was beyond doubt, as from the little pool of sunshine had a mighty ocean grown. Repeatedly peering up at the sun for 2½hr can go a long way towards ruining your eyesight, but to see racing cloud melt, perpetually, as it approached the sun and re-form just beyond it was, to coin a phrase, 'quite phenom'nal!'

Left: Unscrupulous 19th-century railway politics resulted in Brechin, a sizeable market town in the 1840s, being bypassed by the main railway from Aberdeen to the south and being placed at the end of a 3½-mile branch line. But the small terminus there gathered to itself a knot of lines linking it to Forfar and to Edzell, in addition to the original connection to Bridge of Dun and Montrose, to make up a thriving interchange in days gone by. But, with passenger services having ceased in 1952, those days were long gone in August 1966 when dereliction had well and truly set in. Having just arrived with, and slipped off, the only remaining service, a daily goods from Montrose, 'J37' 0-6-0 No 64576 is already busy making up her return train.

Below: In contrast to the view opposite, the last railway scene I was to record in Scotland would have changed little since 1952, the year of my first visit. The photograph depicts the locomotive shed at Alloa with 'J38' 0-6-0 No 65903 the only locomotive on view. It was situated south of the station alongside the line to Dunfermline, whose motive power depot it was an outpost of. The line curving away in the top left of the photograph originally led to Kinross via Crook of Devon, but was now curtailed at Dollar.

Left: Sporting its unique and probably useless smoke deflector and a plain chimney, 'V2' 2-6-2 No 60813, prepared as if for special duty, heads past Broughty Ferry on 6 August 1966, having just taken over a Saturdays-only Blackpool to Aberdeen train at nearby Dundee. This Dundee & Arbroath line, already part of the East Coast main line, was to have added importance the following year when the Glasgow to Aberdeen service, so conspicuously featured in these pages, was routed this way following the severance of the magnificent Caledonian route through Strathmore.

Above: There's that distinctive green cap again, as the fireman of 'A2' No 60532 takes a breather on the downgrade through Bridge of Allan while manning the 1.30pm from Aberdeen on 6 August 1966. All week long *Blue Peter* had soldiered on alone, while the three 'serviceable' streamliners had obstinately remained out of service. They had been thus the previous Saturday so that when, from the TV in the lounge at the 'Drumlithie', *that* voice had famously exclaimed: 'They think it's all over...', it carried a more weighty connotation than the end of a mere football match! Well, history relates that it was not *quite* all over for the 'A4s', but at that moment it was for me: my last ever picture of an ex-LNER Pacific in service, and almost my last in Scotland.

Index to Locations